SCHOLASTIC

VOCABULARY-BUILDING Card Games

GRADE 5

BY LIANE B. ONISH

NEW YORK • TORONTO • LONDON • AUCKLAND • SYDNEY
MEXICO CITY • NEW DELHI • HONG KONG • BUENOS AIRES

Teaching Resources

Hi, Mom!

Editor: Joan Novelli
Cover design by Maria Lilja.
Interior design by Kathy Massaro.
Interior art by Anne Kennedy.

ISBN 13: 978-0-439-57816-5
ISBN 10: 0-439-57816-7

Contents

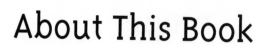

About This Book

Games make learning new words fun and effective. The more words students can recognize easily, the more they will read; and the more they read, the more words they will know, which will make them better and more willing readers, and stronger speakers, spellers, writers, and test takers. This book features 20 exciting, easy-to-make, easy-to-play card games and variations, to help students learn more than 200 words and develop and reinforce valuable vocabulary skills.

Research shows that vocabulary development is highly correlated with overall student success. "Having a strong vocabulary is of particular importance to students in that it contributes significantly to achievement both in the subjects of their school curriculum and also on standardized tests" (Shostak, 2002). Direct instruction and reading widely are both important factors in increasing students' vocabulary. Repeated exposure to words and independent practice with them are also essential, and word games are an effective way to provide these opportunities. The games in this book provide for both the playful approach and level of practice that students need, and can be played again and again to build and deepen word knowledge, strengthen related skills, and make the learning stick.

What the Research Says

"Intuition tells us that more practice leads to better memory. Research tells us something more precise: Memory in either the short- or long-term requires ongoing practice."

(Willingham, 2004)

How Much Practice?

Vocabulary development is an essential part of reading comprehension. The more words we know, the better we comprehend what we read. How much practice is enough to learn new words? "It is difficult to overstate the value of practice. For a new skill to become automatic or for new knowledge to become long-lasting, sustained practice, *beyond the point of mastery*, is necessary" (Willingham, 2004). Research shows that we need about 12 exposures to, or encounters with, a new word before we know it well enough to comprehend it in text (McKeown, Beck, Omanson, & Pople, 1985; as cited in Beck, McKeown, & Kucan, 2002). Playing vocabulary games, as a regular part of classroom activities, gives students the multiple encounters they need to "own" more words.

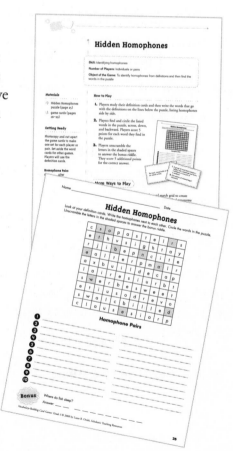

What's Inside?

In addition to 20 word games, you'll find a master list of target words for easy reference, as well as blank game card templates and extra game cards. Here's a closer look at each section of the book.

Pages 9–11: Master Word List

A game-by-game list of words is provided for easy reference. You can also use this list to create speed drill practice for reading fluency and automaticity. (See More Ways to Use the Word Cards, page 7.)

Pages 12–66: Vocabulary Games

Directions for 20 vocabulary-building games follow a simple format to make it easy for students to set up and play.

* **Skill:** All games are designed to build vocabulary. Some games may have additional areas of instructional focus, such as recognizing parts of speech or developing specificity of language in writing.

* **Number of Players:** Games provide opportunities for varied groupings, from one or two students to the entire class.

* **Object of the Game:** How to win varies from game to game.

* **Materials:** In addition to game cards, this section lists any other materials students need to play, such as index cards or a timer.

* **How to Play:** Step-by-step directions make it easy to set up and get started.

* **More Ways to Play:** Suggestions in this section help teachers create simpler or more challenging games to meet the learning needs of different groups of students. This section also features fresh twists on games to keep motivation for learning high and provide for additional practice.

Each game focuses on a particular set of words. For some games, such as Acting Out (page 12) and Root for the Home Team (page 34), target words are specified and reproducible game cards are provided accordingly. For others, such as Take Two (page 33) and Voca-Bees (page 53), you will select the game cards from other games or from the extra game cards (pages 68–80), or use the blank game card templates (page 67) to create your own. For any of the games, you can use the extra game cards and blank game card templates to customize vocabulary.

Teaching Tip

You'll find that many of the games work with cards from other games, as well as with the extra cards. You can also adapt the games for use with specific content area vocabulary. Simply copy the blank game card templates and fill in desired words. Review the game with those words in mind and make any adjustments that might be necessary.

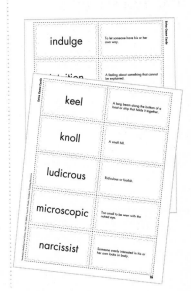

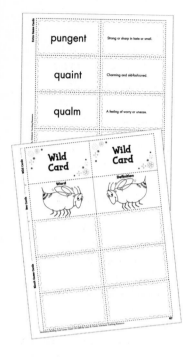

Pages 67–80: Extra Game Cards

These pages feature extra game cards for customizing any game. Use the Wild Cards to put a twist on games such as Take Two (page 33). The Bee Cards, used for Voca-Bees (page 53), can be used to make playful cards for any game. Keep a supply of blank game card templates on hand to customize games as students play. Use the extra word and definition cards for games that specify "any word cards," and to create new game card sets for other games.

Teaching With the Games

You can use the games in any order that best supports your teaching needs. The Contents page (page 3) summarizes specific skills to assist with game selection. Additional information follows for setting up, introducing, and playing the games.

Setup and Storage

Once you choose a game and gather any necessary materials, take a few minutes to set up a storage system. With the setup that follows, students can easily use the games at school as well as transport them home to play with families, reinforcing the connections between home and school that lead to more successful learning.

1. For durability, photocopy the game cards on cardstock, or glue them to index cards and laminate.

2. Clip the cards for each game together (or place them in an envelope) and store in a resealable plastic bag. Consider making a second set of cards for each game as backup. (Place these in an envelope and label "Extra Set of Cards.")

3. Label each bag with the name of the game, the skill it reinforces, and the number of players.

4. Photocopy the directions and tape them to the inside of the bag.

Introducing the Games

Introduce the games one at a time in any order that best matches your language arts program and your students' needs. Model how to play, including for individual players, pairs, small groups, and the whole class. (See Number of Players for each game.) Keep in mind that the games provide support for differentiated learning. Each game includes suggestions for variations, including, for example, using fewer or more word cards and simplifying or increasing the level of vocabulary difficulty. You may also choose games to use with students based on identified needs. Students who need additional practice with easily confused words, for example, will benefit from playing Hidden Homophones

(page 24). Foreign Affairs (page 48) is just right for students who are ready to broaden their vocabulary base with words borrowed from other languages.

Who Goes First?

There are many ways to decide who goes first in a game. Here are a few ideas from which students can choose. Invite them to suggest their own ideas, too.

❉ Have players roll a die. The player who rolls the highest number goes first. The next player is the one sitting clockwise from the first player. For variety, have the player who rolls the lowest number go first.

❉ Use the first initial of each player's name. The player whose name is closest to *A* (or *Z*) goes first, with the other players following clockwise.

❉ Mix up the word cards for the game. Deal one card to each player. The player whose word is closest to *A* (or *Z*) goes first.

More Ways to Use the Word Cards

In addition to using the word cards to play the games in this book, there are many other ways you can use them to provide the practice students need to achieve long-lasting learning. Following are suggestions.

❉ **Daily Word:** Photocopy several sets of cards in this book, but do not cut apart the word-definition pairs. Distribute one word-definition card to each student daily. Have students record the part of speech for each meaning (there are a few definition cards for which this has already been provided as part of the game) and write a sentence for each one on the reverse. Invite them to share their cards as they wish, placing them in a basket for classmates to peruse.

❉ **From *A* to *Z*:** When students prepare to play a vocabulary game, have them first select one of the word cards at random. After reviewing the word and definition, have students play in alphabetical order according to the word on their card.

❉ **House of Cards Stories:** Let students use the game cards to build house-of-cards pyramids. (You may want to glue word cards to index cards for this purpose.) Then have them share their pyramid words with a small group or partner. Challenge them to use all the words in their pyramid in a story. Variations: Build parts-of-speech pyramids using just nouns, verbs, or adjectives, or words that can be both nouns and verbs. Before students use a card in a part-of-speech pyramid, they must write a sentence on it that illustrates the appropriate part of speech.

Bibliography

Beck, I. L., McKeown, M. G., & Kucan, L. (2002). *Bringing Words to Life: Robust Vocabulary Instruction.* New York: The Guilford Press.

Blevins, W. (2006). *Phonics From A to Z: A Practical Guide* (2nd ed.). New York: Scholastic.

Fry, E. B., & Kress, J. E. (2006). *The Reading Teacher's Book of Lists* (5th ed.). San Francisco, CA: Jossey-Bass.

Kamil, M. L., Mosenthal, P. B., Pearson, P. D., & Barr, R. (Eds.). (2000). *Handbook of Reading Research, Vol. III.* Mahwah, NJ: Lawrence Erlbaum Associates.

Shostak, J. (2002). "The Value of Direct and Systematic Vocabulary Instruction." Retrieved September 27, 2007, from www.sadlier-oxford.com/docs/pdf/9147-9_VW_WhitePaper_Vol7.pdf.

Willingham, D. T. (2004, Spring). "Practice Makes Perfect—But Only if You Practice Beyond the Point of Perfection." *American Educator.*

As students revisit games and words, encourage them to use prior knowledge to make new connections. What word parts do they recognize? How can they use what they know to make sense of unfamiliar words? Invite students to suggest synonyms, antonyms, or homonyms for words they encounter in various games. There are games, such as Synonym Slap-Down (page 15), that specifically address these areas, but students can have these discussions with any of the games, building new knowledge each time.

✳ **Curriculum Vocabulary:** Use the blank game card templates to make content area word cards. Provide students with a word card and have them complete a definition card, writing the meaning and using the word in a sentence. Encourage students to use their textbooks or dictionaries for reference. Then use the new set of cards in a game, such as Voca-Bees (page 53).

✳ **Pick a Card, Any Card:** Make a class set of all the word cards and a set of all the definition cards. Keep them in separate boxes or large baskets. Use them by the handful for practice. Read words; have students provide the definitions. Read definitions; have students provide the words.

✳ **Card Collecting:** Give students several blank, uncut word and definition cards (two blank cards side-by-side and uncut) to use as bookmarks for independent reading. Let them select a word from their daily reading to share with a book group. Have them write the word on the left side of the card, the definition on the right, and a sentence of their own or from the book on the reverse.

✳ **Making Up New Games:** Invite students to choose any game cards and create new games to play.

A Note About Word Parts

Learning to break longer words into smaller, recognizable parts is an essential tool for vocabulary development. Of new words a student encounters in reading, approximately 60 percent can be analyzed into parts that provide significant help in determining meaning (Nagy & Anderson, 1984; as cited in Kamil, Mosenthal, Pearson, & Barr, 2000). A study of Greek and Latin roots helps students build knowledge of word parts. Greek and Latin were influential languages, and they contributed roots for many everyday words to other languages. For example, the Greek word *teckhne* meant "something made by human intelligence," and it forms the root of our words *technical* and *technique*.

You can build students' base for comprehension by looking for opportunities as they play the games in this book to point out and teach common Greek and Latin roots. For example, with Root for the Home Team (page 34), when students learn that the Latin root *fract* or *frag* means "break," they can more easily make sense of words that contain this root, such as *fraction, fracture, fragile,* and *infraction.* In Synonym Slap-Down (page 15), students who learn the meaning of the word part *pre* (Latin: "before," "in front") in *prejudice* can use that knowledge to figure out other words they might encounter, such as *prelude* and *preamble.*

chron [root]	Greek root meaning time.
chronic	Going on for a long time, such as a disease, and not getting better.
chronicle	To record historical events in a careful, detailed way.
chronological	Arranged in the order in which events happened.
synchronize	To arrange events so that they happen at the same time or in a certain order.

Master Word List

Acting Out (page 12)

airtight	hand-feed	timeline
coal mine	lighthouse	undertake
drawbridge	living room	
fire-eater	network	

Synonym Slap Down (page 15)

abandon	important
clothes	prejudice
disaster	problem
eager	serious
hub	special

Opposites Attract (page 18)

advance	interrupt
amateur	obvious
continue	particular
damage	professional
definite	retreat
general	superb
hidden	suspect
improve	thorough
incomplete	trust
inferior	vague

Vocabulary Baseball (page 23)

Any words from other games or from the extra game cards (pages 68–80).

Hidden Homophones (page 24)

altar	alter	clause	claws
billed	build	overdo	overdue
brews	bruise	paced	paste
cereal	serial	praise	preys
cite	sight	suite	sweet

Proper Anagrams (page 30)

hasten: Athens (Greece)
more: Rome (Italy)
pairs: Paris (France)
solo: Oslo (Norway)
tooled: Toledo (Spain)

Take Two (page 33)

Any words from other games or from the extra game cards (pages 68–80).

Root for the Home Team (page 34)

astr: asterisk, asteroid, astronaut, astronomical
aud: audience, audition, auditory, inaudible
chron: chronic, chronicle, chronological, synchronize
fract, frag: fraction, fracture, fragile, infraction

Vocabulary Password (page 39)

Any words from other games or from the extra game cards (pages 68–80).

Voca-Bingo! (page 40)

Any words from other games or from the extra game cards (pages 68–80).

A & Q (page 42)

Some (irregular plurals): axes, brothers-in-law, crises, indices/indexes, passersby

Then (irregular past tenses): forbade, meant, slew, understood, wove

Clip It (clipped words): burger (hamburger), champ (champion), dorm (dormitory), gas (gasoline), tux (tuxedo)

Shorties (abbreviations): asst. (assistant), med. (medium), oz. (ounce), pkg. (package), vol. (volume)

A-List Words (words beginning with *a*): accompany, advice, article, attain, awkward

Foreign Affairs (page 48)

bona fide
entre nous
faux pas

persona non grata
pied-à-terre

Definitely in Order (page 50)

deface   defy   delicate
defer   degree   delicious
defiant   delay
deft   delete

Voca-Bees (page 53)

Any words from other games or from the extra game cards (pages 68–80).

Sentence-Ology (page 54)

Any words from other games or from the extra game cards (pages 68–80).

Look! It's a Noun! No, It's a Verb! (page 56)

arch   carp   spray
attack   collar   wake
batter   hack
blind   shed

As You Like It (page 60)

busy as a beaver

clean as a whistle

crazy like a fox

eats like a horse

looks like something the cat dragged in

straight as an arrow

run around like a chicken with its head cut off

thick as thieves

tight as a drum

works like a charm

Mail Call (page 63)

Any words from other games or from the extra game cards (pages 68–80).

Parts of Speech Rummy (page 64)

Nouns: activity, blizzard, caboose, damsel, emperor, faucet, gallon, habitat, industry, jackpot, kennel, lagoon, matrix

Verbs: absorb, backfire, calculate, dampen, eavesdrop, fidget, gallop, halve, imply, jostle, kindle, lengthen, measured

Adjectives: adjacent, belated, capable, decisive, eager, fantastic, greasy, handsome, immature, jumbo, keen, lame, majestic

Adverbs: abruptly, backward, cautiously, dishonestly, eastward, fearlessly, gingerly, hardly, indoors, justly, kindly, legally, meekly

Wish You Were Here (page 66)

Varies.

Extra Game Cards (pages 68–80)

apathetic	jeopardy
artifact	jovial
caper	keel
casualty	knoll
circumvent	ludicrous
compel	microscopic
component	narcissist
conscientious	nuisance
cordial	persistent
decisive	perturb
dichotomy	populous
diminutive	prognosis
docile	pungent
eccentric	quaint
eradicate	qualm
eventual	steed
evident	stodgy
feeble	sustenance
grimace	thespian
grotesque	topical
grounded	unwieldy
gruff	upheaval
haste	utility
heritage	verify
high-strung	versatile
immense	vex
impart	virtue
inclined	waft
incognito	waive
indicate	yearn
indulge	yonder
intuition	zest
jeer	

Acting Out

Skill: Recognizing closed, open, and hyphenated compound words

Number of Players: Teams of 2 or 3 players

Object of the Game: To pantomime compound words for others to guess

Materials

❋ game cards (pages 13–14)

Getting Ready

Photocopy and cut apart the game cards. Save the definition cards for other games.

2 syllables

sounds like feet

seatbelt

belt

How to Play

1. Give each team of two or three players a game card to pantomime.

2. Explain that there are three types of compound words: closed, open, and hyphenated. *Doghouse* is a closed compound word, *swimming pool* is an open compound word, and *hand-me-down* is a hyphenated compound word. Invite players to suggest other examples of each.

3. Establish rules: At the beginning of each charade, the players must identify the number of syllables in the word by raising the appropriate number of fingers. Then they must identify the syllable they will act out first. Players may act out each word, a homophone for one of the words, a rhyme for a syllable or word, or the meaning of the compound. If they choose to act out a word that rhymes with the syllable, they must first touch their ear to indicate "sounds like." Teams may point to, but not touch, people or classroom objects.

4. When another team thinks they know the word, they write it on a sheet of paper and then stand up.

5. The first team to correctly name the pantomimed word goes next. Play until all teams have had a chance to act out their word.

More Ways to Play

❋ **Sticky-Note Charades:** Invite students to look for examples of compound words in their reading and mark them with sticky notes. Later, have them transfer their words to blank game cards (page 67) and use them for a new round of Acting Out.

❋ **Read All About It:** Give pairs of players a page from the daily newspaper. Have players work together to locate and highlight examples of compound words. Display the newspaper pages so students can review words their classmates found.

airtight

Sealed so well that no air can get in or out.

coal mine

A large hole made in the earth to remove a black mineral made from ancient plants that can be burned as fuel.

drawbridge

A bridge that can be raised or moved to let boats pass underneath.

fire-eater

Someone who entertains by appearing to swallow flames.

hand-feed

To feed an animal or a person by hand.

lighthouse	A tower set in or near the sea, with a flashing light on top to guide ships or warn them of danger.
living room	A lounge or sitting room in a home.
network	**1.** A system of things that are connected to one another. **2.** To link computers so that they can work together.
timeline	A schedule or table listing important events over a successive period of time.
undertake	**1.** To agree to do a job or a task. **2.** To set about; to try or attempt.

Vocabulary-Building Card Games: Grade 5 © 2008 by Liane B. Onish, Scholastic Teaching Resources

Synonym Slap-Down

Skill: Identifying synonyms

Number of Players: 4 to 6

Object of the Game: To collect the sets of synonym cards

How to Play

1. Create a slap-down deck with four word cards for each player. For example, for five players, use five sets of four synonym cards, for a total of 20 cards.

2. Mix up and deal the cards, four to each player.

3. Players keep their hand hidden from the others, and select a card they do not want. Explain that the object of the game is to collect four synonym cards.

4. Players place their unwanted card facedown on the table. When all have an unwanted card ready, they slide it to the player on their left at the same time.

5. Players look at their new cards and select another unwanted card to pass as before. Play continues in this way. The first player to get four synonyms and slap the hand on the table is the winner.

6. Other players check the winning hand to see that the four words are synonyms, using the definition cards as needed.

More Ways to Play

* **Fresh, New, Novel:** To keep the game fresh (or add players), add new sets of synonyms. Use the blank game card templates (page 67) to make sets of synonym cards. Use students' writing or reading as a source of words.

* **Which of These Words Is Not Like the Others?** Use the blank game card templates to add distracters. Display sets of cards that include several synonyms and one distracter. Have players identify the incorrect word. Example: For the synonym set for *abandon,* add a card for *dessert.* For the synonym set for *clothes,* add a card for *nearby.*

Materials

* game cards (pages 16–17)
* blank game card templates (page 67)

Getting Ready

Photocopy and cut apart the game cards and blank game card templates (30). Set aside the definition cards for later use in the game. Write the synonyms listed for each game card word on the blank cards (one per card).

abandon: depart, desert, withdraw; **clothes:** apparel, attire, garments; **disaster:** calamity, catastrophe, misfortune; **eager:** avid, enthusiastic, keen; **hub:** center, middle, nucleus; **important:** major, principal, significant; **prejudice:** bias, bigotry, intolerance; **problem:** dilemma, mystery, riddle; **serious:** grave, solemn, somber; **special:** particular, specific, unique.

abandon

1. To leave forever.
2. To give up.
Synonyms: depart, desert, withdraw.

clothes

Things that you wear.
Synonyms: apparel, attire, garments.

disaster

1. An event that causes great damage, loss, or suffering.
2. Something that turns out completely wrong.
Synonyms: calamity, catastrophe, misfortune.

eager

Very interested in doing something; enthusiastic.
Synonyms: avid, enthusiastic, keen.

hub

1. The center of a wheel.
2. The center of an organization or activity.
Synonyms: center, middle, nucleus.

vocabulary-Building Card Games: Grade 3 © 2008 by Liane B. Onish, Scholastic Teaching Resources

important

1. Worth taking seriously because it can have a great impact.
2. Having high social position or influence.

Synonyms: major, principal, significant.

prejudice

A fixed, unreasonable, or unfair opinion, or hatred about someone based on race, religion, or other characteristic.

Synonyms: bias, bigotry, intolerance.

problem

1. A difficult situation that needs to be figured out or overcome.
2. A puzzle or question to be solved.

Synonyms: dilemma, mystery, riddle.

serious

1. Solemn and thoughtful.
2. Sincere or not joking.
3. Very bad or dangerous.
4. Important and requiring lots of thought.

Synonyms: grave, solemn, somber.

special

Different or unusual.

Synonyms: particular, specific, unique.

Vocabulary-Building Card Games: Grade 3 © 2008 by Liane B. Onish, Scholastic Teaching Resources

Opposites Attract

Play outdoors or in an open space

Skill: Identifying antonyms

Number of Players: An even number of players

Object of the Game: To find the player who has an antonym for your word card

Materials

* game cards (pages 19–22)
* blank game card templates (page 67)
* timer

Getting Ready

Photocopy and cut apart the game cards. Save the definition cards for other games. Make enough cards so there is one for each player. Use the blank game cards to add antonym pairs as needed.

How to Play

1. Mix up the cards. Distribute randomly, one word to each player. Tell players not to look at their cards until you say "Go."

2. Say "Go," and start the timer. Players hold up their cards and find the other player who has an antonym for their word.

3. When players pair up, have them sit down. When all players are paired, stop the timer.

4. Note the time. Discuss strategies players could use to pair up faster.

5. Collect the cards, mix them up, redistribute, and play again. Compare times and discuss other strategies.

More Ways to Play

* **Synonym Siblings:** Play with synonym pairs: *astonish-surprise, border-edge, courageous-daring, charm-enchant, country-nation, danger-peril, different-varied, dwell-reside, form-shape, mature-develop.*

* **Find All Four:** Shuffle the word and definition cards, and then arrange facedown in an array. Players take turns flipping over any four cards at a time to find a matching set of antonym cards (two antonym cards and two definition cards).

advance	To move forward; to make progress.
amateur	Someone who takes part in a sport or other activity for pleasure rather than for money.
continue	To go on doing something.
damage	To harm something.
definite	Certain; clear.

general	Not detailed or specialized.
hidden	Concealed from view.
improve	To get better or to make something better.
incomplete	Not finished or not complete.
inferior	Not as good as something else in quality or value.

interrupt	To stop or hinder for a short time.
obvious	Easy to see or understand.
particular	Individual or special.
professional	One who makes money for doing something others do for fun.
retreat	To move back or withdraw from a difficult situation.

Vocabulary–Building Card Games: Grade 5 © 2008 by Liane B. Onish, Scholastic Teaching Resources

superb	Excellent or outstanding.
suspect	To have doubts about.
thorough	Complete in each detail and done with care.
trust	To believe someone is honest and reliable.
vague	Not clear or not definite.

Vocabulary-Building Card Games: Grade 5 © 2008 by Liane B. Onish, Scholastic Teaching Resources

Vocabulary Baseball

Skill: Identifying vocabulary words using definitions

Number of Players: 2 teams

Object of the Game: To run the bases and score by identifying vocabulary words

How to Play

1. Divide the class into two teams. Designate corners of the room as home, first, second, and third bases. The "pitcher," the teacher or a student, sits in the middle of the room.

2. The team "at bat" lines up along the side of the room by home base. The pitcher reads the first definition. If the "batter" correctly identifies the word (with the pitcher checking the back of the card to confirm), he or she goes to first base.

3. Continue reading definitions to new batters. Players move from base to base as batters correctly identify vocabulary words. Players returning to home plate score a point for their team.

4. Each incorrect answer is an "out." When the team at bat has three outs, the second team is up.

5. Play each game for four or more innings. The team with the most points wins.

More Ways to Play

* **What's the Meaning?** Instead of reading definitions, read vocabulary words and have the batters supply the definitions.

* **Singles, Doubles, Triples, and Home Runs:** Divide vocabulary words by difficulty into singles, doubles, triples, and home runs. Batters request a single, double, triple, or home-run word.

Materials

* game cards (any)
* glue

Getting Ready

Photocopy and cut apart any word and definition cards, such as those from Synonym Slap-Down (page 15), or the extra game cards (pages 68–80). Cut apart the cards in such a way as to keep each word and definition pair intact. Fold at the center and glue back-to-back to create flash cards.

Hidden Homophones

Skill: Identifying homophones

Number of Players: Individuals or pairs

Object of the Game: To identify homophones from definitions and then find the words in the puzzle

Materials

❋ Hidden Homophones puzzle (page 25)

❋ game cards (pages 26–29)

Getting Ready

Photocopy and cut apart the game cards to make one set for each player or pair. Set aside the word cards for other games. Players will use the definition cards.

Homophone Pairs

altar	alter
billed	build
brews	bruise
cereal	serial
cite	sight
clause	claws
overdo	overdue
paced	paste
praise	preys
suite	sweet

Answer: on waterbeds

How to Play

1. Players study their definition cards and then write the words that go with the definitions on the lines below the puzzle, listing homophones side by side.

2. Players find and circle the listed words in the puzzle, across, down, and backward. Players score 5 points for each word they find in the puzzle.

3. Players unscramble the letters in the shaded spaces to answer the bonus riddle. They score 5 additional points for the correct answer.

More Ways to Play

❋ **Hidden Words:** Give students a blank word search grid to create new puzzles with other definitions. They can play to find synonyms or antonyms.

❋ **Word Search Time:** After players list the words that match the definition cards, have them estimate how long it will take to find the words, and then time it.

Hidden Homophones

Look at your definition cards. Write the homophones next to each other. Circle the words in the puzzle. Unscramble the letters in the shaded spaces to answer the bonus riddle.

c	s	o	p	a	s	t	e	l	r	s
e	t	h	v	s	i	g	h	t	a	y
r	j	i	b	e	p	n	c	i	t	e
e	a	l	t	e	r	p	m	a	l	r
a	x	b	u	i	l	d	e	c	a	p
l	a	i	r	e	s	i	u	r	b	t
s	w	e	r	b	e	s	w	e	e	t
e	t	i	u	s	o	d	r	e	v	o
s	w	a	l	c	b	i	l	l	e	d
c	l	a	u	s	e	s	i	a	r	p

Homophone Pairs

1. _____   _____
2. _____   _____
3. _____   _____
4. _____   _____
5. _____   _____
6. _____   _____
7. _____   _____
8. _____   _____
9. _____   _____
10. _____   _____

Bonus

Where do fish sleep?

Answer: ___ ___   ___ ___ ___ ___ ___ ___

altar	A large table in a house of worship used for religious ceremonies.
alter	To change something.
billed	To have sent or given someone a piece of paper showing how much money is owed to you for something bought.
brews	To prepare a liquid by steeping, as for coffee or tea.
bruise	A discolored area that you get on your skin when you fall or are hit by something.

Vocabulary-Building Card Games: Grade 5 © 2008 by Liane B. Onish, Scholastic Teaching Resources

build	To make something by putting different parts together.
cereal	A grain crop grown for food, such as wheat, corn, rice, oats, or barley.
cite	**1.** To quote from a written work. **2.** To give someone a commendation or medal. **3.** To use as proof of an argument.
clause	**1.** A group of words that contains a subject and a predicate and forms a sentence or one part of a sentence. **2.** One section of a formal legal document.
claws	The hard, curved nails on the foot of an animal or bird.

overdo

To do too much.

overdue

Past due; late.

paced

1. Measured distance in steps.
2. Walked back and forth.

paste

noun: A soft, sticky mixture used to stick things together.

verb: **1.** To stick with paste. **2.** On a computer, to insert at the cursor text or graphics copied or cut from another location.

praise

noun: Words of approval or admiration.

verb: To shower compliments on someone.

Vocabulary-Building Card Games: Grade 3 © 2008 by Liane B. Onish, Scholastic Teaching Resources

preys

noun: Animals that are hunted by another animal for food.

verb: Robs, attacks, or takes advantage of someone who is helpless or unable to fight back.

serial

A story that is told in several parts.

sight

noun: **1.** The ability or act of seeing. **2.** The range or distance a person can see. **3.** A view or a scene. **4.** A small metal device on a rifle that helps in aiming. **5.** Something funny or odd to look at.

verb: To see or to spot.

suite

1. A group of rooms that are connected. **2.** A set of matching items. **3.** A piece of music made up of several parts.

sweet

adjective: **1.** Tasting of sugar or honey. **2.** Pleasant in taste, smell, or sound. **3.** Gentle and kind, good-natured.

noun: A piece of candy or other food that tastes sweet.

Proper Anagrams

Skill: Rearranging letters to make new words (anagrams)

Number of Players: Individuals or pairs

Object of the Game: To rearrange the letters of words to spell new words

Materials

* game cards (pages 31–32)
* envelope
* map of Europe (optional)

Getting Ready

Photocopy and cut apart a set of game cards (letter cards and clue cards) for each player or pair of players. Place each set of letter cards in an envelope.

Answers
hasten: Athens (Greece)
more: Rome (Italy)
pairs: Paris (France)
solo: Oslo (Norway)
tooled: Toledo (Spain)

How to Play

1. Distribute a clue card facedown to each player or pair of players. Give each player or pair of players a set of letter cards.

2. Players turn over their clue card and use the letter cards to spell the word that answers the first clue. Players write the answer on their cards, then use the same letter cards to answer the other clue on the card.

3. Repeat for each clue card.

4. Optional: Have students find the cities on a map of Europe.

More Ways to Play

* **Hidden Anagram:** Write a sentence that contains an anagram on a whiteboard. Challenge players to find the word, and come up with the anagram. For example: "That bowl of ice cream looks delicious." (The letters in *bowl* can also be used to spell *blow*.)

* **Class Clues:** Invite pairs of players to write a set of clues for a new anagram. Have teams exchange clues and use their letters to spell the answers. (Use the blank letter cards as needed to add extra letters to the set.)

H	E	R	O	T
P	A	L	A	O
S	I	S	R	S
O	D	O	T	L
M	E	N	O	E

Anagram Clue Card 1

1. The capital of Italy.

_____

2. Not as much as most, not as little as some.

_____

Anagram Clue Card 2

1. The capital of France.

_____

2. Groups of two things that match.

_____

Anagram Clue Card 3

1. The capital of Greece.

_____

2. To move quickly.

_____

Anagram Clue Card 4

1. The capital of Norway.

_____

2. Done by one person.

_____

Anagram Clue Card 5

1. A city near the capital of Spain.

_____

2. To have imprinted a design on a book with a stamp.

_____

Take Two

Skill: Matching words and their definitions

Number of Players: 2 or more

Object of the Game: To collect the most sets of words and definitions

How to Play

1. Mix up the cards and place them facedown in a 9 x 6 (minus two) array.

2. Play as you would play Concentration. The first player turns over two cards. If the cards show a word and its definition, the player keeps the pair and turns over two more cards. If the two cards do not match, the player turns them facedown and the next player takes a turn.

3. If one or more of the cards is a Wild Card, the player may say or write a word or definition to make a pair.

4. The winner is the player with the most pairs at the end of the game.

More Ways to Play

※ **Mini-Maxi Wordy Concentration:** Use fewer or more sets of word and definition cards.

※ **Fill-In Concentration:** Use 20 vocabulary words cards, just 15 matching definition cards, and 5 Wild Cards.

※ **Synonym, Antonym, or Homophone Concentration:** Use synonym, antonym, or homophone pairs in place of words and definitions.

Materials

※ game cards (any)
※ Wild Cards (page 67)

Getting Ready

Photocopy and cut apart any 25 word cards and their definitions, plus two Wild Cards, for 52 cards total.

Root for the Home Team

Play outdoors or in an open space

Skill: Identifying vocabulary words and their roots by definitions

Number of Players: 1 or 2 players, or a group of 20

Object of the Game: To group vocabulary words by their Greek or Latin roots

Materials

❉ game cards (pages 35–38)

❉ 4 envelopes

❉ glue

Getting Ready

Photocopy and cut apart the game cards (roots, words, and definitions). Place each set of definition cards in an envelope. Glue the matching root card to each envelope.

Teaching Tip

Encourage players to notice how the meaning of the words that go with each envelope are alike. How does this word part help them understand the meaning of each word?

How to Play

One or Two Players:

1. Place the envelopes at the far end of a table.

2. Give players a set of word cards. Players sort cards into four groups according to common roots (*astr, aud, chron, fract/ frag*).

3. After cards are sorted, players find the envelopes with the matching definition cards, and then match words to definitions.

Group Play:

1. Place the envelopes in the four corners of the room or playing area.

2. Give each player a word card. When you say "Go!" players find the classmates who have word cards for the same root.

3. When players find their group, the group then finds the envelope with the matching definition cards. Players match their word cards to corresponding definition cards.

More Ways to Play

❉ **Time to Root:** Time individual players, pairs, or groups. Repeat and compare.

❉ **Root Raps:** Each group makes up a rap or cheer for their root using the word cards and other words with the same root.

astr (root)

Greek root meaning star.

asterisk

The mark (*) used in print to tell readers to look elsewhere on the page for more information.

asteroid

A planet-like object that travels around the sun.

astronaut

Someone who travels in space.

astronomical

1. Having to do with the study of stars, planets, and space.
2. Very large.

aud (root)

Latin root meaning hear.

audience

1. The people who watch or listen to a performance, speech, or movie.
2. A formal meeting with an important or powerful person.

audition

A short performance by an actor, singer, musician, or dancer to see whether he or she is suitable for a part in a play, concert, etc.

auditory

Related to or through hearing.

inaudible

Not loud enough to be heard.

chron (root)	Greek root meaning time.
chronic	Going on for a long time, such as a disease, and not getting better.
chronicle	To record historical events in a careful, detailed way.
chronological	Arranged in the order in which events happened.
synchronize	To arrange events so that they happen at the same time or in a certain order.

fract, frag (root)

Latin root meaning break.

fraction

1. A part of a whole number; part of a whole.
2. A small amount.

fracture

To break or crack something, especially a bone.

fragile

Delicate, or easily broken.

infraction

A failure to obey a rule, law, contract, or agreement.

Vocabulary Password

Skill: Identifying vocabulary words from definition clues

Number of Players: Pairs

Object of the Game: To name as many vocabulary words as possible in one minute

How to Play

1. Mix up the cards. Divide the cards into two piles.

2. Play as you would play Password. Player 1 looks at the first vocabulary word without showing it to player 2. When player 1 is ready, start the timer. Player 1 gives clues without using the word. Player 2 tries to guess the word. When player 2 correctly identifies the word, he or she gets the card. Either player may say "Pass" to move on to the next word.

3. Play continues for one minute.

4. Players switch roles and use the second pile of word cards. The pair scores one point for each correct word identified.

More Ways to Play

* **Flipping for Words:** Mix up the word cards and arrange them faceup in an array. Set a timer for three minutes. When you say "Go," player 1 gives clues to a word and player 2 locates it and flips it over. Players continue this way until time is up, and then count the number of cards they flipped. Players trade places, and continue, trying to flip all the cards in another three-minute period.

* **Attribute Password:** Rather than giving meaning clues, have players give attribute clues, describing features of words, such as "This word begins with the same letter as *kayak*. It has a double vowel in the middle."

Materials

* game cards (any)
* minute timer

Getting Ready

Photocopy and cut apart 20 word cards for each pair of players. Set any definition cards to the side for other games.

Voca-Bingo!

Skill: Identifying vocabulary words from definitions

Number of Players: Any

Object of the Game: To color five words in a row going down, across, or diagonally

Materials

※ game board (page 41)

※ game cards (any)

※ crayons or light markers

Getting Ready

Photocopy and distribute a game board to each player. Photocopy and cut apart 24 word and definition cards (such as those from the extra game cards, pages 68–80). Use more than 24 words to allow players some choice in the words they include on their game board.

How to Play

1. Make two piles, one for words, one for definitions.

2. Play as you would play Bingo. Read each word aloud. Have players write each word in any space on their game board. To allow players to pass on some words, read more than 24 words. Let students know ahead of time how many words they can pass on altogether. For example, if you select and read 30 words, students can pass on any 6 of them.

3. Read a definition. Players look for the word that goes with the definition on their game boards. Then players use their crayons or markers to shade in the box. Continue reading the top definition card and setting it aside until one player has five words in a row, horizontally, vertically, or diagonally, and calls, "Voca-Bingo!"

More Ways to Play

※ **Syno-Bingo or Anto-Bingo:** Use synonyms or antonyms in place of definition cards.

※ **All the Way Around:** Play until one player has every word around the outside of the board (16 in all). Or, play to make an X from the corners through the center or stripes filling the first, third, and fifth rows or columns.

※ **It's Free!** Make a 4 x 4 bingo board for a simpler game. Let students designate a free space anywhere on the board.

Voca-Bingo!

		Free! Gratis! Complimentary!		

A & Q

Skill: Identifying vocabulary words from meaning clues

Number of Players: 3 to 5 individuals, or 3 teams of 2 players each

Object of the Game: To collect the most cards

Materials

❋ game cards (pages 43–47)

❋ 5 envelopes

❋ clickers or other noisemakers

Getting Ready

Photocopy and cut apart the game cards. Do not separate word cards from the matching definition cards (leave center line between each word card and definition card intact). Place each set of cards in an envelope and write the category name on it: Some (irregular plurals), Then (irregular past tenses), Clip It (clipped words), Shorties (abbreviations), and A-List Words (words beginning with a).

How to Play

1. Explain categories to players. Play as you would play Jeopardy. Rules: The first player will choose a category. The teacher or other leader will select a card from that category's envelope and read the definition. When any player knows the answer, he or she signals using a clicker or other noisemaker. The first player to signal gives the answer, phrased as a question. For example, if the clue is "To gain or achieve," a player might answer, "What is to *attain*?" If the answer is correct, the player gets the word card and selects the next category. For words with more than one definition, players may use any one meaning in their answer.

2. If the player is incorrect, other players may signal with their clickers. The first player to signal gives the answer, also phrased as a question. If correct, the player gets the card and selects the next category.

3. The winner is the player (or team) with the most cards at the end of the game.

More Ways to Play

❋ **A & Q & S:** Players must correctly spell answers to receive the word card.

❋ **Create a Category:** Use vocabulary words from single or multiple subjects to create new categories. For example:

Book Parts: *acknowledgment, dedication, glossary, jacket, spine*

S as in Social Studies: *sabotage, sanction, Senate, surplus, sweatshop*

G as in Geography: *geyser, glacier, grasslands, greenhouse effect, gulf*

The I's Have It: *icon, idle, ignite, immune, incision*

Travel: *cable car, kayak, pram, space shuttle, tricycle*

axes	**1.** More than one imaginary line through the middle of objects, around which the objects spin. **2.** The lines at the bottom of a graph.
brothers-in-law	The brothers of someone's spouse, or the husbands of someone's sister.
crises	Times of danger or difficulty.
indices/indexes	Alphabetic listings that show where to find things in books.
passersby	More than one person who happens to be walking by.

forbade	To have ordered someone not to do something.
meant	**1.** To have tried to express. **2.** Intended to do something.
slew	To have killed in a violent way.
understood	**1.** To have known what something means or how it works. **2.** To have known very well. **3.** To have had sympathy for someone.
wove	**1.** To have made cloth, baskets, and other objects by passing threads or strips over and under each other. **2.** To have spun a web or cocoon.

burger

A short or clipped word for *hamburger*: A flat piece of cooked meat, usually served on a bun.

champ

A short or clipped word for *champion*: The winner of a competition or tournament.

dorm

A short or clipped word for *dormitory*: A building with many separate sleeping rooms.

gas

A short or clipped word for *gasoline*: A liquid fuel made from oil used in many vehicles.

tux

A short or clipped word for *tuxedo*: A man's jacket, usually with satin lapels, worn with a bow tie for formal occasions.

asst.

Abbreviation for *assistant*:
A person who helps someone else
do a task or job.

med.

Abbreviation for *medium*:
Average or middle.

oz.

Abbreviation for *ounce*:
A unit of measure equal to $\frac{1}{16}$ pound.

pkg.

Abbreviation for *package*:
A parcel, or a bundle of something
that is packed, wrapped, or put into
a box.

vol.

Abbreviation for *volume*:
1. A book. **2.** Loudness.

accompany

1. To go somewhere with someone.
2. To support a musician or singer by playing along on a musical instrument.

advice

A suggestion about what someone should do.

article

1. An object or a thing.
2. A piece of writing published in a newspaper or magazine.
3. A word, such as *a*, *an*, or *the*, that goes in front of a noun.

attain

To gain or achieve.

awkward

1. Difficult or embarrassing.
2. Not able to relax and talk to people easily.

Foreign Affairs

play outdoors or in an open space

Skill: Understanding and using French and Latin idioms

Number of Players: Groups of 3

Objective: To write cloze sentences for foreign idioms and match idioms to sentences

Materials

❋ game cards (page 49)

❋ blank game card templates (page 67)

Getting Ready

Photocopy and cut apart the game cards, making enough so that each group of players will have an idiom card and its matching definition card. Use duplicate cards, or add other idioms, if necessary. Photocopy and cut apart a blank game card for each group of players.

Teaching Tip

An idiom is an expression that can't be directly translated, i.e., its meaning can't be directly derived from its parts but is known through common usage. The idioms used in this game fit within a broader definition of idiom that includes expressions particular to certain regions.

How to Play

1. Discuss the meanings of common French idioms, such as *a la mode, du jour,* and *bon voyage.* Have volunteers use each in a sentence.

2. Give each group of players a set of cards (idiom, definition, and blank card). Have players write a cloze sentence for their idiom on the blank card.

3. Collect and mix up the idiom, definition, and cloze sentence cards.

4. Distribute one card to each player. Players do not look at their cards until you say "Go!" They then find their classmates who have the matching cards.

5. The winner is the first group to find all its members.

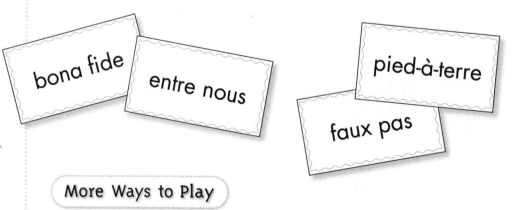

More Ways to Play

❋ **Picture This:** Replace sentence cards with picture cards. Have players draw pictures to explain the meaning of the idioms. Collect, shuffle, and redistribute the cards. Have students locate their matches.

❋ **Spill the Beans:** Replace French and Latin idioms with English idioms. Examples include *down to the wire, butterflies in your stomach, spill the beans, neck and neck,* and *ants in your pants.*

bona fide

(**bow**-na fide)
(*Latin:* in good faith)
1. Genuine or sincere.
2. In good faith, or without fraud.

entre nous

(ahn-tra **noo**)
(*French:* between us)
Confidentially.

faux pas

(foh **pah**)
(*French:* false step)
An embarrassing social blunder.

persona non grata

(per-so-nah non **grat**-ah)
(*Latin:* person not accepted)
1. Not welcomed.
2. An unacceptable person.

pied-à-terre

(pee-ay-duh-**tare**)
(*French:* feet to the ground)
A small home or apartment to use when you are visiting the town or city.

Definitely in Order

Skill: Alphabetizing to three letters

Number of Players: 1 or 2 players, or teams of 10

Object of the Game: To arrange vocabulary words in alphabetical order

Materials

* game cards (pages 51–52)
* timer (optional)
* table or whiteboard tray (for teams)

Getting Ready

Photocopy and cut apart the game cards. Make one set per player or team. Set aside the definition cards for variations and other games.

How to Play

One or Two Players:

1. Give a set of cards to each player. Set the timer for three minutes.

2. Players arrange the cards in alphabetical order. At the end of three minutes, players count the number of cards in correct alphabetical order.

3. Option: Do not use a timer. Play to correctly alphabetize all cards.

Teams:

1. Mix up a set of cards and stack facedown in front of each team. Teams line up some distance from their playing field.

2. The first player takes the top card and runs to the team's playing field. The player places the card about where it should go in alphabetical order. For example, the word *deface* should be placed on the far left of the playing field, the word *delicious* on the far right. The player runs to the back of the line.

3. Each player adds one card to the team's playing field, and rearranges the cards as needed.

4. The winner is the first team to accurately place their cards in order.

More Ways to Play

* **Order the Definitions:** Use the definition cards and the word cards. Arrange word cards on a table or whiteboard tray. Give teams the mixed-up definition cards. Players must find the word that matches their definition, and then place the definition card on top.

* **Words In Order:** Use a handful of randomly selected vocabulary word cards for individuals, pairs, or teams to alphabetize.

deface	To spoil the way something looks by writing on it, scratching it, etc.

defer	1. To put something off until later. 2. To give in to another's wishes or opinions.

defiant	Standing up to someone or to some organization and refusing to obey.

deft	Skillful, quick, and neat.

defy	1. To refuse to obey. 2. To challenge or dare someone to do something.

degree

1. A step in a series.
2. A unit for measuring temperature.
3. A unit for measuring angles.
4. A title given by a college or university.

delay

1. To be late.
2. To make someone or something late.
3. To put off something until later.

delete

To remove something from a piece of writing or computer text.

delicate

1. Very pleasant to the senses.
2. Finely made or sensitive.
3. Not very strong; can easily become ill.

delicious

Very pleasing to taste or smell.

Voca-Bees

Skill: Spelling, defining, and using vocabulary words in sentences

Number of Players: Whole class or large group

Object of the Game: To correctly spell, define, and use the words in sentences

How to Play

1. Mix up the cards and place in a pile, word-side up.

2. Divide the group into two teams. Have teams line up on opposite sides of the room.

3. Read the top word for team 1. The first player in team 1 repeats the word, spells it, tells what it means, and uses it in a sentence. If the player is correct, the player gets the Bee Card. If the player is incorrect, the first player on team 2 can answer.

4. Read the next word for the first (or next) player on team 2.

5. Continue as above until all players on both teams have played.

6. The winner is the team that collects the most cards.

More Ways to Play

✳ **Define-a-Bees:** Read the definition, not the word. Players identify and spell the word that goes with the definition.

✳ **Bee Mine:** Give each player a blank bee word and definition card. Have players select a word from their independent or subject area reading and create a new game card. Collect the cards and use in later games.

✳ **Buzz Off:** Divide the group into four "hives." Identify a queen or king bee for each hive to give the words to the other players. The winner in each hive (player to collect the most cards) is the new queen or king bee. The four queen and king bees play the Buzz Off round. Players in the Buzz Off may consult their hive members for help.

Materials

✳ Bee Cards (page 67)

✳ game cards (any)

✳ glue or paper clips (optional)

Getting Ready

Photocopy and cut apart the Bee Cards; do not cut the word and definition sides apart. Fill in the cards with words and definitions from other games or from the extra game cards. Fold each word and definition card in half. If desired, glue backs together or paper-clip to secure. Prepare as many game cards as there are players.

Sentence-Ology

Skill: Using vocabulary words in sentences

Number of Players: 4

Object of the Game: To create sentences using two or more vocabulary words

Materials

* scorecards (page 55)
* game cards (any)
* die (or spinner with numbers 1–6)
* dictionary

Getting Ready

Photocopy a scorecard for each player. Photocopy and cut apart 30 word cards from other games, such as Opposites Attract (page 18) and A & Q (page 42), or the extra game cards (pages 68–80).

How to Play

1. Each player takes a scorecard. Mix up the word cards and place in a pile. Set aside definition cards for later use. One player acts as the dealer.

2. The first player rolls the die. The dealer gives the player that many word cards. (Players who roll a 1 roll again.) The next player rolls the die, and so on until all players, including the dealer, have their cards.

3. Players write a single sentence trying to use all their word cards in that one sentence. When all players are finished, the first player reads his or her sentence aloud. If the other players agree that the sentence makes sense, and that all vocabulary words have been used correctly, the player scores the sentence according to the scoring guidelines on the scorecard. (See Scoring, page 55.) All players read and score their sentences.

4. If a player challenges the sense of a sentence, or the use of a vocabulary word, the group discusses the challenge. The dealer checks the definition card or consults the dictionary. If the sentence is successfully challenged, the player must replace it. The challenger receives a bonus of 5 points.

5. The dealer collects all the cards, and mixes them up. Then the dealer passes the cards to the player on his or her left to be the new dealer for round two. Repeat until all players have four sentences on their scorecards and everyone has been the dealer.

6. Players total their points. The winner is the player with the highest score.

More Ways to Play

* **Defy, Delay, Defeat:** Create a set of game cards using words that begin with the same letter sound. Have players use them to make alliterative sentences.

Sentence-Ology Scorecard

Sentences	Number of Words	Word Cards Used	3+ Syllables
1			
2			
3			
4			
Subtotals			
Grand Total			

Vocabulary-Building Card Games: Grade 5 © 2008 by Liane B. Onish, Scholastic Teaching Resources

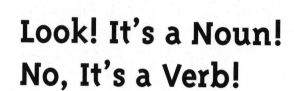

Look! It's a Noun!
No, It's a Verb!

Skill: Using vocabulary words as different parts of speech

Number of Players: Teams of 10

Objective: To use words as specified parts of speech in complete sentences

Materials

❋ game cards (pages 57–59)

❋ glue

❋ index cards

❋ box or basket

❋ tables or whiteboards (or markers and chart paper)

Getting Ready

Photocopy and cut apart a set of word and definition cards for each team. Glue to index cards. Photocopy and cut apart one set of the parts-of-speech cards. Mix up these cards and place in a box or basket. Set aside the definition cards to be used to check sentences and for use with other games.

How to Play

1. Divide the class into teams of ten. Provide each team with a playing field (a whiteboard or markers and chart paper) in a different corner of the room. Teams line up in the middle of the room.

2. Each team gets a set of word cards, mixed up and placed facedown.

3. When the teacher says "Go," the first player on each team takes the top card and runs to the team's playing field. At the same time, the teacher picks a random parts-of-speech card from the box, reads it aloud, and places the card back in the box.

4. Players write a sentence using their word card as the designated part of speech, adding affixes to the base word as needed. After writing their sentences, players check spelling and punctuation, circle the word in the sentence, and write *N* (noun) or *V* (verb) after the sentence.

5. The next player on each team takes the next word card, runs to the team's board or chart as the caller reads the next parts-of-speech card, and repeats the procedure.

6. Make definition cards available for teams to check one another's sentences. Each correct sentence scores 10 points. Each word in each correct sentence adds 1 point to the total. The winner is the team with the highest score.

More Ways to Play

❋ **Look! More!** Use the blank parts-of-speech cards to make two Adjective parts-of-speech cards. Add words that can be used as both nouns and adjectives, such as *compound, fresh, off, own,* and *rash.*

❋ **Is It a Noun? Is It a Verb?** Read aloud a game-card word and then use it in a sentence. Have players or teams compete to be the first to identify the part of speech.

arch

noun: A curved structure.

verb: To curve.

attack

verb: **1.** To try to hurt someone or something. **2.** To criticize strongly.

noun: A sudden period of illness.

batter

verb: **1.** To injure someone by hitting repeatedly.

noun: **1.** A baseball or softball player whose turn it is to bat the ball.
2. A mixture of mainly milk, eggs, and flour used to make baked goods or used to coat food before frying.

blind

verb: To make unable to see.

noun: A window shade made of stiffened cloth, metal, or other material.

carp

noun: A kind of freshwater fish.

verb: To find fault with someone or something; complain.

collar

noun: The part of a shirt, blouse, coat, etc., that fits around your neck.

verb: To catch someone.

hack

verb: To chop or cut roughly.

noun: **1.** A short, dry cough.
2. (informal) Taxi, or car, for hire.

shed

noun: A small building or shelter used for storing things.

verb: **1.** To let something fall or drop.
2. To get rid of.

spray

verb: To scatter or sprinkle liquid in very small drops.

noun: A small branch with leaves and flowers.

wake

verb: To become fully conscious after being asleep.

noun: **1.** A watch kept over the body of a dead person before a funeral.
2. The trail of ripples in the water left by a moving boat or something passing through.

Look! It's a verb!

No, it's a **noun!**

Look! It's a verb!

No, it's a **noun!**

Look! It's a noun!

No, it's a **verb!**

Look! It's a noun!

No, it's a **verb!**

As You Like It

> **Skill:** Completing similes and creating new ones
>
> **Number of Players:** Pairs, or groups of 3
>
> **Object of the Game:** To match simile puzzle pieces with their definitions and write new figures of speech

Materials

✳ game cards (pages 61–62)

✳ envelopes

Getting Ready

Photocopy and cut apart the game cards. Cut apart each simile card vertically along the dashed line. Place three or four sets of simile pieces and definitions in an envelope. Prepare an envelope for each group for players.

Teaching Tip

Encourage students to remember that the words *like* and *as* are clues that can help them recognize when similes are being used. When they encounter a simile, identifying the two things being compared will help them understand what is being communicated.

How to Play

1. Explain that a simile is a comparison using the words *like* or *as*. Share an example: *clear as day.* Discuss the meaning of the simile. Then discuss the simile *clear as mud,* pointing out how this comparison vividly describes a lack of clarity.

2. Give one envelope to each group. Players find the pieces to complete each simile and its definition.

3. As a team, players write three or four more similes of their own using one or more key words from their simile puzzles.

4. Groups share their similes. Let the class vote for the best, using a variety of categories, such as: most descriptive, most original, funniest, longest, and shortest.

5. Players select their favorite similes to illustrate.

More Ways to Play

✳ **Missing-Simile Sentences:** Vary the game by substituting sentences for definitions. Leave blanks for either the noun or adjective part of the simile. Write the missing parts on blank word cards. (Examples: In the library, she was as _____ as a mouse. In the library, she was as quiet as a _____.) Give students sentences and word cards and have them put them together. For a challenge, include several distracter word cards.

✳ **As Good as Gold:** Give students blank game card templates and let them make a new version of the game, using similes they already know or encounter in their reading. Examples include: *as slow as molasses, as easy as ABC,* and *fits like a glove.*

busy as	a beaver	Hardworking and industrious.
clean as	a whistle	Completely; entirely; thoroughly.
crazy like	a fox	Appearing foolish, but actually cunning and very shrewd.
eats like	a horse	Eats a lot.
looks like	something the cat dragged in	Looks completely bedraggled.

run around like	a chicken with its head cut off	To behave in a crazy, frenzied, or distracted way.
straight as	an arrow	Honest; sincere.
thick as	thieves	Closely associated or allied with.
tight as	a drum	Close-fitting; taut; watertight.
works like	a charm	Functions very well; causes the hoped-for effect or outcome.

Vocabulary-Building Card Games: Grade 5 © 2006 by Liane B. Onish, Scholastic Teaching Resources

Mail Call

Skill: Identifying vocabulary words

Number of Players: Small groups or whole class

Object of the Game: To use clues to identify a vocabulary word

How to Play

1. Select the first player to receive the "mail."

2. Choose a vocabulary word card. Pass it around so that all other players can read the word. Include the definition card, if desired, so players can check their knowledge of the word.

3. Place the word card in the envelope and deliver it to the player.

4. Play as you would play 20 Questions. You may want to give the player a clue, such as identifying the subject area from which the word was chosen. The player with the mail asks questions to try to identify the word. Each question the player asks must have only a yes or no answer. Sample questions: "Is it a proper noun?" "Is it a person?" "Is it a place in the Western Hemisphere?" "Is it a river?" "Does it have four syllables?"

5. When the player has enough information and guesses the word, he or she opens the envelope to check the answer. The student who gave the final clue becomes the next player to receive mail.

More Ways to Play

❋ **Content Area Mail Call:** Create new game cards using content area vocabulary. For a challenge, reduce the number of allowed questions to ten.

❋ **Mail of Interest:** Select game cards according to a topic of interest to students, such as sports, music, or movies.

Materials

❋ game cards (any)
❋ envelope

Getting Ready

Photocopy and cut apart any game cards, such as those from Look! It's a Noun! No, It's a Verb! (page 56) or from the extra game cards (pages 68–80).

Parts of Speech Rummy

Skill: Identifying parts of speech and alphabetizing

Number of Players: Groups of 4 to 6 players

Object of the Game: To get rid of all of one's cards

Materials

❈ game cards (page 65)

Getting Ready

Photocopy and cut apart multiple copies of the cards. Write the following words on them (one word per card), using one pattern for each part of speech:

Nouns: activity, blizzard, caboose, damsel, emperor, faucet, gallon, habitat, industry, jackpot, kennel, lagoon, matrix

Verbs: absorb, backfire, calculate, dampen, eavesdrop, fidget, gallop, halve, imply, jostle, kindle, lengthen, measured

Adjectives: adjacent, belated, capable, decisive, eager, fantastic, greasy, handsome, immature, jumbo, keen, lame, majestic

Adverbs: abruptly, backward, cautiously, dishonestly, eastward, fearlessly, gingerly, hardly, indoors, justly, kindly, legally, meekly

How to Play

1. Mix up the cards. For four players, deal each player seven cards. For five or six players, deal six cards each. Place the remaining cards facedown in a pile. This is the stockpile. Turn over the top card and place it next to the pile. This is the discard pile.

2. Players organize the cards in their hand, placing any melds of three or four cards on the table. A meld is three or four cards beginning with the same letter (such as *activity*, *absorb*, and *adjacent*), or three or four cards that are the same part of speech and are also in alphabetical order (such as *activity*, *blizzard*, and *caboose*).

3. Play as you would play Rummy. The first player takes the top card from the stockpile, or the card in the discard pile. Then the player places any melds from his or her hand on the table. To end the turn, the player discards a card from the hand, placing it faceup on the discard pile.

4. The next player takes a card from either the stockpile or the discard pile. If the player has a meld, he or she puts it on the table. Each turn ends with the player discarding a card.

5. The winner is the first player to get rid of all his or her cards.

More Ways to Play

❈ **More Rummy:** Challenge students to create their own Parts of Speech Rummy decks of 13 words in alphabetical order

❈ **Wacky Sentences:** Place cards by parts of speech in bags (all nouns in one bag, all verbs in another, and so on). Have players take turns selecting one card from each bag, and then putting the words together in a sentence. Players may change the form of a word as necessary (for example, changing *lengthen* to *lengthens*).

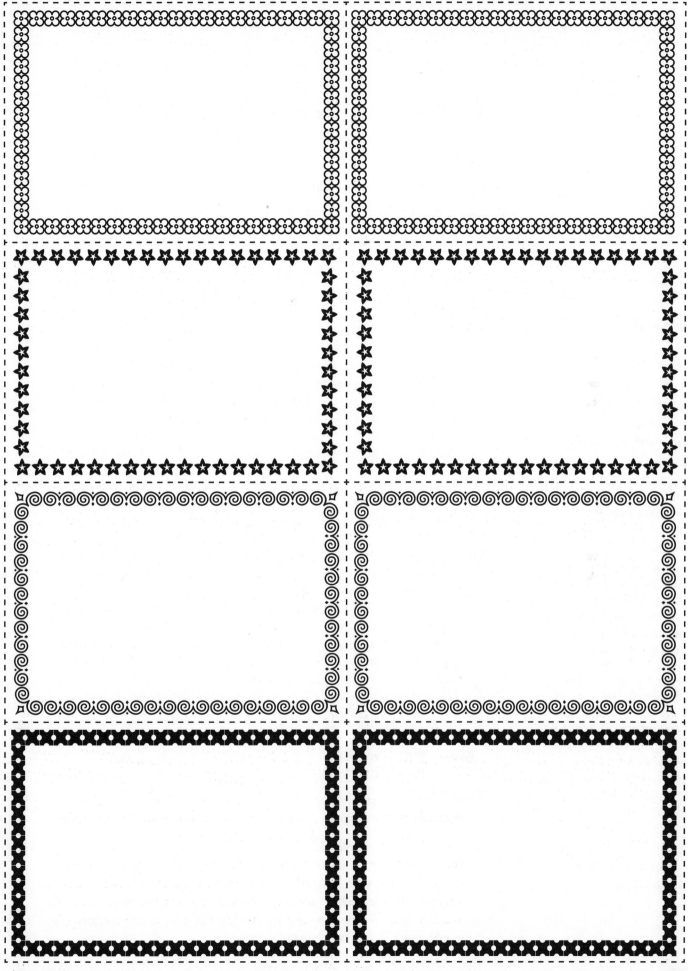

Wish You Were Here

Skill: Brainstorming specific language for details

Number of Players: Pairs, or groups of 3

Object of the Game: To list word and phrases that describe pictures

Materials

※ picture postcards or magazine photographs

※ paper and writing materials

※ timer

Getting Ready

Collect interesting, colorful postcards, magazine photographs, or illustrations. Use as many pictures as there are groups. Number the back of each picture.

Teaching Tip

Look for opportunities with this game to review parts of speech. For example, have students examine the words they use to describe the pictures and tell what part of speech they are. Are certain types of words most useful for descriptions?

How to Play

1. Distribute a picture, illustration-side down, to each group of players. Teams write the number of the picture on the top of a sheet of paper.

2. Set the timer for one minute. When you say "Go" players list words and phrases to describe details in their picture. At the end of the one minute, players stop writing.

3. Players pass their picture to a neighboring team, so each team has a new picture. Repeat step 2. Play until all teams have played a round with each picture.

4. Scoring: Choose a picture and a team to read words for that picture. If other groups have the same word or phrase for that picture, all teams cross the word off their lists. Only unique words or details score points. Repeat for each picture and team, again having teams cross off any duplicated descriptions. Teams may challenge others to explain, defend, or point out the detail as described. Players score 5 points for each unique description.

5. The winner is the team with the most points for each picture.

More Ways to Play

※ **Picture Perfect:** Have students collect pictures to use for the game. Place them in a box or envelope for use with other writing activities.

※ **It's All in the Details:** Choose new pictures. On blank game cards (page 67), write details that describe the pictures. Choose words that are as specific and descriptive as possible. Mix up the cards and pictures. Let players decide which words go with each picture and tell why.

Wild Card

Wild Card

Word

Definition

| apathetic | Not caring about anything or wanting to do anything. |

| artifact | A simple object, such as a tool or decorative object, made or modified by hand, especially a tool or weapon from the past. |

| caper | A mischievous trick or prank. |

| casualty | Someone injured or killed in an accident, a disaster, or a war. |

| circumvent | 1. To make a circuit around.
2. To manage to get around by clever means. |

compel	To make someone do something by giving him or her orders or by using force.
component	A part of a whole, such as a machine or system.
conscientious	Making sure to do things well and thoroughly.
cordial	Warm, friendly, or gracious.
decisive	Making choices quickly and easily.

dichotomy	A division of something into two usually conflicting groups.
diminutive	Tiny or very small.
docile	Calm and easy to manage or train.
eccentric	Acting odd or strange, in a harmless or charming way.
eradicate	To get rid of something completely, especially something bad, such as disease, crime, or poverty.

eventual	Final, or happening at last.
evident	Clear and obvious.
feeble	Very weak.
grimace	A facial expression usually indicating a negative reaction.
grotesque	Very strange or ugly.

grounded	**1.** Unable to fly, as an aircraft. **2.** (*informal*) Not allowed to go out.
gruff	Rough or rude.
haste	Speed or quickness in moving or acting.
heritage	Valuable or important traditions handed down from generation to generation.
high-strung	Very nervous or excitable.

Vocabulary-Building Card Games (Unit 3) © 2008 by Liane B. Onish, Scholastic Teaching Resources

immense	Huge or enormous.
impart	**1.** To share or communicate knowledge or information. **2.** To give something a particular quality.
inclined	**1.** Leaning or sloping. **2.** Likely or tending to do something.
incognito	Disguising one's identity, by wearing something or using a different name.
indicate	**1.** To show or prove something. **2.** To point out something clearly.

indulge	To let someone have his or her own way.
intuition	A feeling about something that cannot be explained.
jeer	To scorn someone in a loud, unpleasant way.
jeopardy	The risk of loss, harm, or injury.
jovial	Cheerful; to enjoy talking and laughing with others.

Vocabulary Building Cards Chunks, Grade 3 © 2005 by Liane B. Onish, Scholastic Teaching Resources

keel	A long beam along the bottom of a boat or ship that holds it together.
knoll	A small hill.
ludicrous	Ridiculous or foolish.
microscopic	Too small to be seen with the naked eye.
narcissist	Someone overly interested in his or her own looks or body.

nuisance	Someone or something that is annoying and causes problems.
persistent	Continuing despite problems or difficulties.
perturb	To upset or confuse.
populous	Numerous or densely populated.
prognosis	The chances of recovery from an illness.

pungent	Strong or sharp in taste or smell.
quaint	Charming and old-fashioned.
qualm	A feeling of worry or unease.
steed	A horse, especially a spirited one.
stodgy	1. Very dull or boring. 2. Old-fashioned and very stuffy.

| sustenance | Food or nourishment that gives strength or support. |

| thespian | An actor. |

| topical | 1. Made for local application or treating a body part. 2. Referring to topics or news of the day. |

| unwieldy | Difficult to hold or hard to manage because of its size, shape, weight, or other complexity. |

| upheaval | 1. A sudden and violent upset or disturbance. 2. A forceful lifting up of part of the earth's crust during an earthquake. |

utility

1. A basic service supplied to a community, such as telephone, water, gas, or electricity.
2. A company that supplies a basic utility.
3. Usefulness.

verify

To prove to be correct or true.

versatile

1. Going easily from one skill to another.
2. Having many uses.

vex

To annoy or irritate.

virtue

1. Moral goodness.
2. An example of moral goodness.
3. Any good quality or trait.

waft	To float or be carried through the air, as if by a breeze.
waive	**1.** To give up something by choice. **2.** To postpone or to set aside.
yearn	To wish or long for something very strongly.
yonder	Over there.
zest	Enthusiasm and liveliness.